ANTON CHEKHOV'S

# THE
# SEAGULL

# The Seagull

Based on the play by Anton Chekhov

Cover photo by Melissa Adams

ISBN-13: 978-1944540418
ISBN-10: 1-944540415

For information about production rights, e-mail:
ad@michiganshakespearefestival.com

Published by Sordelet Ink
WWW.SORDELETINK.COM

ANTON CHEKHOV'S

# THE
# SEAGULL

TRANSLATED FROM THE RUSSIAN BY
ALEXANDRA LACOMBE

ADAPTED FOR THE STAGE BY
JANICE L BLIXT

SORDELET
ink

**The Seagull** received its world premiere at the Michigan Shakespeare Festival on July 16, 2017. It was directed by Janice L Blixt. Costume design was by Darice Damata-Geiger; lighting design was by David Staughton; scenic design was by Jeromy Hopgood; properties design was by Sara Shearer; original music and sound design was by Kate Hopgood. The production stage manager was Stefanie Din. The cast was as follows:

Arkadina - Janet Haley *
Trigorin - Shawn Pfautsch *
Sorin - Lee Palmer *
Constantine - Ian Gears
Nina - Lauren Grace Thompson
Shamraev - Tobin Hissong *
Polina - Vanessa Sawson
Masha - Risha Tenae
Medvedenko - Christopher L. Martin
Dr Dorn - Alan Ball *
Yakov - Eric Eilersen

* - denotes member of Actor's Equity Association

The following credit must appear in all programs/playbills handed to audience members at performances of *The Seagull*:

THIS TRANSLATION OF *THE SEAGULL* WAS ORIGINALLY PRODUCED BY THE MICHIGAN SHAKESPEARE FESTIVAL IN 2017.

# Cast of Characters

ARKADINA (Dina) – Irina Nikolayevna Arkadina, 45 – a famous stage actress, beautiful, clever.

TRIGORIN – Boris Alexeyevich Trigorin, 40 – Arkadina's lover, a famous writer, brilliant, impractical.

SORIN – Pjotr Nikolayevich Sorin, 60 – Arkadina's brother, a respected Wall Street financier, retired.

CONSTANTINE – Konstantin Gavrilovich Treplev, 25 – Arkadina's son, an aspriring playwright, a dreamer.

NINA – Nina Mikhailovna Zarechnaya, 20 – Constantine's love, neighbor girl, aspiring actress, scattered, flakey, but kind and hopeful.

SHAMRAYEV – Ilya Afanasyevich Shamrayev – Sorin's estate manager. A "townie" – respected, but disapproving of the "artist" lifestyle.

POLINA – Polina Andreyevna Shamrayeva – Shamraev's wife. Townie girl, had ambitions, settled for life. Loves Dorn.

MASHA – Ilya and Polina's daughter. Smart, biting, resigned. Would love for Constantine to notice her, doesn't expect it to ever happen.

MEDVEDENKO – Semyon Semyonovich Medvedenko – local townie schoolteacher, loves Masha, Supports his family, a good, yet boring man.

DR. DORN – Yevgeny Sergeyevich Dorn – local doctor, friend of the family. 55. Educated, well traveled, flirts with the women, has an affair with Polina, can't be tied down.

YAKOV – works on the estate – neighborhood guy, not the brightest.

# Setting

An Estate in Upstate New York, 1890s

# ADAPTOR'S NOTE

I have one very strict rule about producing plays: I will never produce a show I don't want to see.

There are many brilliant plays out there that intrigue me artistically that I won't produce, because I think the process would be more fun than the product. It's largely a matter of taste and personal aesthetics. But art shouldn't be done for the artists. Theatre does not become art until the audience is involved.

I'm not alone in this. I know many theatre artists who feel this way, especially about Chekhov. They want to get in there and play with the characters, find the beats, make it all work. But don't ask them to go see a production. They'll complain about self-indulgent, "good for you" theatre.

My answer is that they probably haven't actually seen Chekhov at all.

Allow me to explain. We all know, of course, that Chekhov wrote in Russian. When we see his plays produced in English, there's another playwright's voice involved. It's not just Chekhov. It's Chekhov *and* Bristow, Chekhov *and* Hampton, Chekhov *and* Stoppard, Chekhov *and* Schmidt, Chekhov *and* Dunnigan... you see my point.

I have been fortunate to have been involved with several terrific (and very funny) productions of

Chekhov's plays, and I had long wanted to produce the amazingly deep and painful humor of *The Seagull*, so edgy and modern in its biting energy.

So I went on an odyssey of *The Seagull* reading. I read more and more translations, yet just couldn't find exactly what I was looking for. So many seemed to make the ensemble characters—Masha, Polina, Dr. Dorn—boring, one-dimensional, and wallpaper-y while making Trigorin a horrid loudmouth who always just talks and talks and *talks* just to hear his own voice and opinions. Worse, they make Constantine and Nina insipid victims and Arkadina an evil villain, flouncing and destroying lives with equal glee.

While there were similarities between all of the translations, there were also many differences, both in terms of characterization and communication.

Which lead me to wonder what Chekhov actually wrote.

I have the great good fortune of being friends with Alexandra Chistyakova LaCombe—lawyer, world traveler, Russian expatriate, and theatre lover. When I announced wanting to do *The Seagull* for 2017 season at the Michigan Shakespeare Festival, she groaned and asked "WHY? It's so boring!"

However, she was my closest Russian-speaking friend. When I asked her to do a line-by-line translation, let's just say she was less than enthused. Nevertheless she dove in, producing a literal translation, without excess or padding. If the character said in Russian, "It's cold," that's what she gave me.

She also admitted she'd only ever read or seen the plays in English—but when reading for the first time in the original, she laughed on every page.

When I got her script, it was amazing. The first thing I noticed was that it was twenty percent shorter than any translation I've ever seen. It was quick, moving, and very modern.

Then I set my work. One major change I made was moving it to upstate New York rather than Russia. This wasn't a whim, but because Alexandra had given me context for some of the jokes. Rather than a Russian name with no meaning, if we say that Nina is performing in Bridgeport, it gets a laugh. So I changed some allusions for an American audience to recognize, and basically made sure the jokes worked and the staging made sense.

Then we began rehearsals. From the first day, I was open with the company in terms of the text: if they found a better way to say something, we looked at it and made decisions together. From Trigorin's exasperated speech about inspiration to a couple of Yakov one-liners, the entire company labored to make the moments honest and true.

I can't tell you this version is somehow "pure." I won't say I'm producing Chekhov without another voice attached. In fact, you'll hear more voices than ever—Chekhov, LaCombe, Blixt, Ball, Eilersen, Geers, Haley, Hissong, Martin, Palmer, Pfautsch, Sawson, Tenae, and Thompson.

What I will say is that we crafted a version of *The Seagull* that is brand new, completely fresh, and retains as much of the intentions of the original script as possible.

It's Chekhov as you've never read him before. And I promise it's a show I'd want to see.

Janice L. Blixt
Artistic Director
Michigan Shakespeare Festival

# ACT I

*(MASHA is sitting and reading in the fading light.*
*MEDVEDENKO is trying to get her attention)*

MEDVEDENKO
Why do you always wear black?

MASHA
I am in mourning for my life.

MEDVEDENKO
For what reason? *(Thoughtful)* I don't understand... You are healthy, your family, though
not wealthy, has means. I have it much harder
than you. I get only twenty-two cents an hour...
and they also subtract for taxes, and I am not in
mourning.

MASHA
Money is not the issue. Even a beggar can be
happy.

MEDVEDENKO
That's the theory, but the practice is more like
this: I, my mother, and my two sisters and my
brother, we live on my salary, and my salary is
only twenty-two cents an hour, which ends up
being about three hundred dollars each year.

Don't I need to eat and drink? Don't I need tea with sugar? Don't I need tobacco? Yes. So I keep hustling. Mourning—I have no time for mourning.

MASHA
The play will start soon.

MEDVEDENKO
Yes. The Play. The play that was written by Constantin, and Nina will act in it. And they are in love with each other, and today their souls will merge in the urge to create the same artistic vision. Isn't that beautiful. *(Pause)* But my soul and your soul do not meet or merge at any point. I love you, I cannot sit at home and avoid my yearning. Every day I walk six miles here and six miles back, I come to my job and I am happy to see you, but I meet with only indifference from you. This is understandable. I am without means, I only make twenty-two cents an hour; I have a large family to support... Who would want to marry me?

MASHA
Nonsense. Your love... touches me, I know it's there. But I cannot respond because... I really don't care. It's as simple as that. *(Offers cigarette)* Smoke?

MEDVEDENKO
No. Thank you.

MASHA
You keep talking about money, money and wages and money and obligations. According to you, there is nothing worse than poverty, than not having money, but I think it is a thousand times

easier to have no money, to walk around in rags and beg than to be without... Nevermind. There's no way you'll understand.

*(Enter SORIN and CONSTANTINE)*

SORIN
I never have nor never will feel like myself in the country—and I will never get used to it. Last night I went to sleep at ten, and this morning I woke up at nine with such a feeling that from a long sleep my brain stuck to my skull and all that. And after dinner I fell asleep again by accident and now I am just all undone and feel, finally, like a nightmare...

CONSTANTINE
True, you need to live in the city. Excuse me, excuse me. Look. You will be called when it is time to start, but now you should not be here. Go away... please.

SORIN
Masha, dear girl, be so kind, ask your father to untie the dog. She barks all night. My sister could not sleep again—and one does not want to be with my sister when she has not slept.

MASHA
You need to talk to him, I'm not going to. Please excuse me.

MEDVEDENKO
Send someone to tell us when it's going to start.

SORIN
So, again, the dog will bark all night. Here is the situation, I have never enjoyed living in the country the way I expected to. It used to be, I

took a vacation from Wall Street for a few weeks and came here to relax, to get away from my life. But now I am attacked with all sorts of nonsense that I want to get out of here the moment I arrive—now my escape from my life *is* my life. I had always left this place with memories of pleasure, relaxed and happy... But, now I am retired, and I have no choice, I am here... Finally... Permanently. I suppose whether you want to or no, you have to live somewhere...

*(Enter YAKOV in a bathing suit)*

YAKOV
I'm going swimming, Constantine.

CONSTANTINE
Fine, but places in ten minutes. It's starting soon.

YAKOV
Understood.

CONSTANTINE
So this is our theater. This would be the "curtain," then foreground, then background, and then empty space. No set. The view opens right to the lake and to the horizon. The curtain goes up at eight thirty sharp, when the moon rises.

SORIN
Wonderful.

CONSTANTINE
If Nina is late, then of course the whole effect will be lost. Fuck. She should already be here. Fuck. Her father and stepmother are guarding her and it is as hard for her to escape that prison of a house.

SORIN
Why is 'Dina is a foul mood?

CONSTANTINE
Why? She is bored. She is anxious. She is jealous.
She was against me, and against the performance,
and against my play, because she is does not have
the part but Nina does. She hasn't even read the
script, but already hates it.

SORIN
You are making this up...

CONSTANTINE
She is already annoyed, that Nina, and not she, will
have attention on this tiny stage. Psychological
curiosity, my mother. Undeniably talented, beautiful, smart, she's capable of crying over a book,
she memorizes entire poems by Wordsworth,
Pushkin, Baudelaire, she takes care of the sick
like an angel of mercy. But, holy shit, try to
praise another actress in front of her! When it
comes to my mother, you can praise only her,
write about only her, scream, rage, obsess, adore
only her and her incomparable acting, but since
there is nothing to give her the same fix here in
the country, she is bored and angry, all of us are
her enemies, and all of us are blamed.

SORIN
You are deciding that your mother doesn't like
your play, and are already worried, that's all.
Calm down, your mother adores you.

CONSTANTINE
(Picking a flower from a planter, he starts pulling off
petals) Loves me—doesn't love me, loves me—

doesn't love me, loves me—doesn't love me. See, my mother doesn't love me. Of course! My mother wants to live, to love, to wear sexy clothes, but I am already twenty-five, and I constantly remind her that she is no longer young. When I am not around, she is only thirty-two, but when I am there, she is forty-five, and she hates me for it. She also knows that I despise her "theater." She loves her theater, she thinks that she serves mankind and the sacred art, but in my opinion, modern theater is a basic superstition. When the curtain rises, with the evening light, in the room with three walls, these great talents and oracles of the sacred art show how people eat, drink, love, walk, wear their skins; when from the vulgar acts and phrases they try to pull a moral—a moral that is small, acceptable, useful at home; when from a thousand variations they keep presenting me with the same, then I run and run, as Maupassant ran from the Eiffel Tower, which crushed his brain with its vulgarity.

SORIN
We can't live without art. Without entertainment. Without theater.

CONSTANTINE
We need new forms of connection! New forms of storytelling! New forms are needed, and if we do not have them, for fuck's sake, we are better off without anything. I love my mother, I love her very much; but she leads a ridiculous life, she runs around with this director, that producer, this writer, her name is constantly bandied about in the newspapers, and it exhausts me. Sometimes

I just feel the egotism of a mere mortal. I feel sorry for myself that my mother is a famous actress, and I feel that I would be happier if she were ordinary. Uncle Sorin, what could be more desperate and more stupid? Sometimes all her guests are all famous artists and writers, designers and thinkers, and only I among them—I am a nothing, and they tolerate me only because I am her son. But who am I? What am I? I dropped out after three years of college because – well, I tell people—circumstances beyond my control—but it was simply that I have no talent. While my father may have been a well-known actor, I am just me. So, when in her presence all these artists and writers and creators deign to pay attention to me, I felt that they are merely measuring my nothingness—I guessed their thoughts and suffered from the insult...

SORIN
By the way, tell me, what kind of man is this writer-fellow of hers? I can't figure him out. He is always so quiet.

CONSTANTINE
He is smart, down to earth, but a little, you know, melancholy. He is... decent. He around forty, but is already famous and respected. His writing? Well... what can I say? Charming, talented... but... after Kipling, Crane, or Henry James, you will not want to read Trigorin.

SORIN
I love literary folk. My dear boy, once upon a time, there was a time when I passionately wanted two things. One, to get married, and two, to be a literary person. I managed neither one.

Yes. I think at the end of the day, it would be pleasant even to be a small literary person.

CONSTANTINE
The air changes, I hear her steps... I cannot live without her... Even the sound of her steps is wonderful... I am insanely happy. My enchantress, my dream...

*(Enter NINA, running)*

NINA
Sorry! Sorry! Sorry! I am not late... Please tell me I am not late...

CONSTANTINE
No, no, no...

NINA
I worried all day, I was so frightened! I was afraid that my father will not let me come... But he just left with my stepmother. The sky is red, the moon is already rising, and I urged my legs to go faster! But I'm here. And now I am alive!

SORIN
You have tears in your eyes... Hey, that's not good!

NINA
That's just... See, I can hardly breathe. Constantine, in half an hour I have to leave, we must hurry. I cannot, I cannot, for God's sake, I cannot be late! My father doesn't know I am here.

CONSTANTINE
Ok—ok—that's fine, we need to start. I'll go call everyone in.

SORIN
I will go get them. This very instant. *(Singing)*
*Frere Jacques, Frere Jacques, dormez vous? Dormez*
*vous?* Do you know, I started singing like this
one time, and a lowly assistant manager told me,
"You, Sir, have a rather strong voice." Then he
thought about it and added, "But an unpleasant
one..." *(Exits)*

NINA
My father and my stepmother would not let me
come here. This place, they say, is full of liber-
als. They say that there is bohemian life here,
that there are no morals, and they are afraid that
I will get into acting. But I feel a pull, like a
seagull to a lake. My heart is full of you.

CONSTANTINE
We are alone.

NINA
I think someone is there...

CONSTANTINE
There is no one.

NINA
Why is it so dark?

CONSTANTINE
It's evening already, everything is getting darker.
Don't leave early, I beg you.

NINA
I cannot.

CONSTANTINE
What if I come to you, Nina? I will stand in your
garden all night long and throw pebbles at your

window?

NINA
You cannot, security will notice you. And the
dogs aren't used to you and will bark.

CONSTANTINE
I love you.

NINA
Shhh...

*(YAKOV enters, heading towards the house)*

CONSTANTINE
Is that you, Yakov?

YAKOV
That's right.

CONSTANTINE
*(Looking at his watch)* Shit. Places. It's time.
Wait—is the moon rising?

YAKOV
Isn't it?

CONSTANTINE
Is there alcohol? Did you set up the sulphur?
When the red eyes appear, it must smell of sulphur.
Go, everything is ready. Are you nervous?

NINA
Yes! Your mother—she is fine, I know her—I am
not afraid of her, but you have Trigorin.... I am
terrified to act in front of him.... My god—a
famous writer... Is he young?

CONSTANTINE
Not really.

NINA
His stories are just marvelous—amazing!

CONSTANTINE
I wouldn't know, I haven't read them.

NINA
Do you know, it's difficult to act in your play. It has no real people.

CONSTANTINE
Real people! Real people? We have to express life not as it is, and not as it should be, but as it comes to us in dreams.

NINA
Your play has no action, only discourses. No plot... And I think that a play must always have love in it...

*(Enter POLINA and DORN)*

POLINA
It's getting damp. Go back, put on your wellies.

DORN
I'm hot.

POLINA
You don't take care of yourself. This is stubbornness. You are a doctor and know perfectly well that damp air is dangerous to you, but you want me to suffer—you just want me to worry. Yesterday you sat out all evening on the terrace on purpose...

DORN
*(Singing)* "By the light of the silvery moon..."

POLINA
You were so involved in a conversation with Arkadina that you did not notice the cold. Tell the truth, you like her...

DORN
I am fifty-five.

POLINA
Nonsense, that's not old for a man. You are very well-preserved and are still attractive to women.

DORN
So what do you want me to do?

POLINA
All of you are ready to bow down before the actress. All of you!

DORN
If artists are loved in society and are treated differently than, say, merchants or bankers or accountants, it's to be expected. It's idealism.

POLINA
Women always fell in love with you and chased after you. Is that also idealism?

DORN
I'm a doctor. *(Beat)* Yes, women have always treated me well. But I was loved primarily for being an excellent doctor. Some ten—maybe fifteen years ago, you remember, I was the only decent obstetrician in the region.

POLINA
My love!

DORN
And I was always an honest man. Quiet. They

are coming.

(*Enter* SHAMRAEV, ARKADINA, *and* TRIGORIN)

SHAMRAEV
Pauline Markham acted magnificently at the Paramount in Newark. Sheer brilliance! She acted splendidly! But do you happen to know, where is the comedian Digby Bell? He was inimitable in The Mikado, better than Lely, I swear to you, esteemed lady. Where is he now?

ARKADINA
The people you are asking about are positively antediluvian. How should I know?

SHAMRAEV
Lew Bloom! They don't make them like him anymore. The stage has collapsed, Arkadina. There used to be mighty oaks, and now we see only stumps.

DORN
True, we have few dazzling talents these days, but the average actor is much improved.

SHAMRAEV
I cannot agree with you. But, that's a matter of taste. "*Malum quam bonum saporem saporem gignit nummos praeter plura.*"

ARKADINA
Constantine, my love, when will it start?

CONSTANTINE
In a minute. Patience, please.

ARKADINA
The time is out of joint...

CONSTANTINE
O cursed spite, that ever I was born to set it right.
Ladies and gentlemen! Your attention, please! I
am starting. O you, revered old shadows who
chase at night above this lake, put us to sleep and
let us dream of what will be in 200,000 years!

SORIN
There will be nothing in 200,000 years.

CONSTANTINE
So let them show us this nothing.

ARKADINA
Let them. We are asleep.

NINA
People, lions, eagles and quails, horned stags,
geese, spiders, silent fish inhabiting the waters,
stars of the sea and those invisible to the naked
eye, in other words, all lives, all lives, all lives,
having completed their sad circle, went out...
Already thousands of centuries since the earth
does not contain any living beings, and this poor
moon lights its lamp in vain. Cranes no longer
wake crying in the meadows, and the beetles
are not heard in the linden groves. It's cold,
cold, cold. It's empty, empty, empty. It's frightening, frightening, frightening. The bodies of
living beings disappeared in the ash, and eternal matter turned them into rocks, into water,
into clouds, and their souls merged into one.
I am the common soul of the world. It is I... I
am the soul of Alexander the Great, and Caesar,
and Shakespeare, and Napoleon, and the lowli-
est worm. In me, the consciousness of humans
merged with the instinct of animals, and I

remember everything, everything, everything, and I live each life anew within myself.

ARKADINA
Ooo. Symbolism.

CONSTANTINE
Mom!

NINA
I am lonely. Once every hundred years, I open my mouth to speak, and my voice sounds dreary in this void, and no one hears... And you, pale lights, do not hear me. Like a prisoner thrown into a deep empty well, I do not know where am I and what awaits me. The only thing not hidden from me is that in the determined and cruel battle with the devil, the beginning of material forces, I am destined to win, and after that the matter and spirit will unite in beautiful harmony and the kingdom of the will of the world will begin. But that will be only after, little by little, after a long, long row of millenniums, the moon and the bright Sirius and the earth will turn into dust... And until then horror, horror... Here approaches my mighty adversary, the devil. I see his awful blood red eyes...

ARKADINA
I smell sulphur. Am I supposed to smell sulphur? Constantine—is it supposed to be like this?

CONSTANTINE
Yes.

ARKADINA
Oh... well... then that's some effect...

**CONSTANTINE**
Mom!

**NINA**
He is bored without humans…

**POLINA**
You took off your hat. Put it back on, or you will catch cold.

**ARKADINA**
The doctor took off his hat to the devil, the father of eternal matter.

**CONSTANTINE**
The play is over! Enough! Stop!

**ARKADINA**
Why are you angry?

**CONSTANTINE**
Enough! Stop! We're done! Sorry! I neglected to note that only the selected few can write plays and act on stage. I violated the monopoly! I insulted the artistic plutocracy! I… I…

*(CONSTANTINE storms out)*

**ARKADINA**
What's with him?

**SORIN**
Dina, you should not treat a young man's ego like this.

**ARKADINA**
But what did I say?

**SORIN**
You hurt his feelings.

ARKADINA
Wait—he set it up like a joke, and so I treated it
like a joke.

SORIN
But still...

ARKADINA
Now it turns out that he wrote a masterpiece! Oh,
please! So, he created this drama—this thing—
and perfumed everything with sulphur not as a
joke, but as a demonstration... As a lesson? He
brought us out here to teach us how plays should
be written and acted? This is becoming boring;
his constant attacks and assaults on me! Spoiled,
self-absorbed boy!

SORIN
He wanted to please you.

ARKADINA
Really? Yet somehow he did not choose a classical play, or some established piece of theatre,
but made us listen to these ravings? I am ready to
listen to ravings as a joke, but here he pretends
to create new forms, some new era in art. But in
my opinion, there are no new forms here, just
the vain ravings of a bad tempered child.

TRIGORIN
Everyone writes as they want and as they can.

ARKADINA
Let him write as he can and as he wants, but let
him leave me out of it.

DORN
You really are angry.

ARKADINA
I am not angry! I am just disappointed that my
son spends his time being so pretentious and
boring. I did not mean to hurt his feelings.

MEDVEDENKO
No one has any basis to separate spirit from matter,
because maybe, the very spirit is a combination
of material atoms. Here is an idea, you know, to
describe in a play and then to act out on stage
the life of a teacher. It is a hard, hard life!

ARKADINA
Let's not talk about art or atoms. It's such a
wonderful evening. Do you hear music? It's so
lovely!

POLINA
It's on the other bank.

ARKADINA
Sit next to me. Ten, fifteen years ago, here on
this lake, you could hear music and singing
almost every night. There are six manor houses
on this shore. I remember laughter, noise,
shots, and romances, ah the romances... And
the heartthrob of all six manor houses was,
here, I am telling you, our own Dr. Dorn. He
is still charming now, but back then, he was
irresistible. *(Beat)* Shit. Why did I have to go
and hurt his feelings? Dammit. Constantine!
Honey—

MASHA
I will go look for him.

ARKADINA
Please, my dear.

MASHA

Hey, Constantine! *(Exits in the direction CONSTANTINE went)*

NINA

Apparently there will be no continuation of the show? And I can come out. Hi! Hello!

SORIN

Bravo! Bravo!

ARKADINA

Bravo! Bravo! We were enjoying you. With such looks, such marvelous voice, it is a sin to be stuck in the country. You are so talented. You hear me? You must go on the stage!

NINA

Oh, that's my dream! But it will never happen.

ARKADINA

Who knows? Please let me introduce to you Trigorin—

NINA

Oh, I am so honored! I read you all the time...

ARKADINA

Don't be embarrassed, my dear. He is famous, but he is a simple soul. See, you have made him embarrassed as well.

DORN

I suppose we can pack this up. Otherwise, it's just a bit sad.

SHAMRAEV

Yakov—come help clean up!

NINA
Isn't it an odd play?

TRIGORIN
I didn't understand anything. But nonetheless, I enjoyed it. Your acting was so sincere. And the setting was wonderful. I should think there are a lot of fish in this lake.

NINA
Yes.

TRIGORIN
I love fishing. I have no greater joy than to sit on a bank in the evening and stare at the bobber.

NINA
But, I think, he who felt the joys of creating art has no other joy in life.

ARKADINA
Don't say that. When you pay him compliments, he is just lost.

SHAMRAEV
I remember once at the Metropolitan Opera, Emma Abbott sang the high C. At this time, as luck would have it, a soprano from our church singers sat in the gallery and you can imagine our incredulity when we hear "Bravo, Emma!" from the gallery, but an octave higher! Like this, "Bravo, Emma..." The entire theater just froze.

DORN
And the angel of silence flies by.

NINA
It's time for me to go, good-bye.

ARKADINA
Where? It's so early. We won't let you go.

NINA
My father is waiting.

ARKADINA
He is such a… Well, what can we do. I am so sorry; sorry to let you go.

NINA
If you only knew, how hard it is to leave!

ARKADINA
Someone should see you home, my girl.

NINA
Oh, no, no!

SORIN
Please stay! I'll talk to your father—

NINA
I can't.

SORIN
Just stay one hour longer, and that's it. Why not, really…

NINA
I can't! *(Exits at a run)*

ARKADINA
Basically, she is a tragic figure. They say, Nina's late mother left her entire—and huge—estate to her husband, down to the last penny, and left nothing to her daughter—the girl is completely without support as the father already willed everything to his second wife. It's outrageous.

DORN
Yes, her father is quite the gargoyle, to give him
his full due.

SORIN
Let's go in, folks, as it's becoming damp. My legs
hurt.

ARKADINA
Your legs are like wood, they barely move.
*(Tenderly)* Let's get you in, you old man.

SHAMRAEV
Wife?

SORIN
I hear that poor dog barking again. Shamraev,
please be so kind, order her untied.

SHAMRAEV
I cannot, Sorin, I am afraid that thieves will get
into the barns. I have millet in there. Yes, a whole
octave higher. "Bravo, Emma!" And not even a
professional singer, just a simple church soloist.

MEDVEDENKO
And what is the salary of the church soloist?

*(They all exit, leaving DORN alone with his ciga-
rette)*

DORN
I don't know, maybe I don't understand anything,
or lost my mind, but I liked the play. There is
something about it. Just a young girl talking
about loneliness and being all alone—and later,
when she talked about the devil's red eyes, my
hands were shaking from emotion. It was fresh,
innocent...

*(Enter CONSTANTINE)*

CONSTANTINE
Everyone's left already?

DORN
I am here.

CONSTANTINE
Masha's looking for me all over the park. What
a little pest!

DORN
Constantine, I liked your play tremendously. It
is kind of strange, and I did not hear the ending,
but it still leaves a strong impression. You are
talented, you need to continue with this. Well,
so emotional. Tearful... What am I trying to say?
You chose an abstract subject matter. That's how
it should be, because an artistic endeavor must
express some big ideas. Only that which is seri-
ous is beautiful.

CONSTANTINE
So you say to continue like this?

DORN
Yes... but express only that which is important and eternal. You know, I have lived my life
enjoying great variety and excitement, and now
I am content, but if I could have been fortunate enough to experience the lift of the spirit
which comes to artists during the creative
process, I think I would have despised the material comforts and would have soared from earth
farther into the heights.

CONSTANTINE
Sorry, where is Nina?

DORN

And another thing. A creative work must contain a clear, specific thought. You must know the purpose of your writing, or you will follow the pretty path without a determined goal and will get lost and your talent will destroy you.

CONSTANTINE

Where is Nina?

DORN

She went home.

CONSTANTINE

I want to see her... I need to see her...

DORN

Calm down, my friend.

CONSTANTINE

But I gotta go.

MASHA

Constantine , get inside the house. Your mother is waiting for you.

CONSTANTINE

Tell her that I left. And I beg all of you, leave me alone! Don't follow me!

DORN

But, dear boy... this isn't...

CONSTANTINE

Good bye, doctor. Thank you. *(Exits)*

DORN

Ah... youth!

*(MASHA enters)*

MASHA
When there is nothing to say, they say, ah youth…

*(Discomfort)*

DORN
I think they are playing in the house. We should go in.

MASHA
Wait—

DORN
What?

MASHA
I want to say something to you. I want to talk… I don't like my father, but I feel affection toward you. For some reason I feel with my entire soul that you are close to me. Please help me. Help me. I'm sure I will do something stupid… I will make a mockery of my life or I will destroy it. I can no longer…

DORN
What? How can I help?

MASHA
I hurt. No one, no one knows how I hurt! I love Constantine.

DORN
How highly strung you all are! How highly strung. And so much love… Oh, enchanted lake! But what can I do, my child? What? What?

*(Lights fade)*

### END OF ACT ONE

# ACT II

*(On the veranda of the house, mid-morning)*

DORN
*(Reading)* "And, of course, it is as dangerous for a person of society to attract and indulge romance writers as for a grain-keeper to raise rats in his barns."

ARKADINA
Let's stand up. Let's stand next to each other. So you are twenty-two years old, and I am almost twice that. Doctor, which one of us is more youthful?

DORN
You, of course.

ARKADINA
Yes, and why? Because I work, I feel, I am constantly engaged, I am alive—and you just sit in one spot, you are not living. And I have a rule never try to see the future. I never think about tomorrow—I never think about getting old or about death. You cannot avoid that which is meant to be, so why think about it?

MASHA
And I have a feeling that I was born a long, long

time ago; I am dragging my life like a useless train of a dress. And often I have no will to live.

DORN

*(Singing)* "I don't care, I don't care, what people think of me..."

ARKADINA

In the papers, they write that I maintain a perfect shape and am always dressed and groomed *comme il faut.* Think about it. Have I ever allowed myself to leave the house, even to go to the garden, in a robe or unkempt? Never. That's why I am beautiful, because I was never a slob, never let myself go like some, because I meet the living of beauty with beauty. It keeps me young... If asked, I can still play fifteen year olds.

DORN

Well, nonetheless I am continuing. We stopped at grain-keepers and rats.

ARKADINA

And rats. Keep reading. Actually, give it to me, I will read, it's my turn. And rats... Here it is... *(Reading)* "And, of course, it is as dangerous for a person of society to attract and indulge romance writers as for a grain-keeper to raise rats in his barns. And yet they are loved. So, when a woman has chosen a writer whom she wants to fulfill her, she besieges him with compliments, flatteries, and indulgences..." Well, maybe *en France,* but not on this side of the pond. Here, a woman, before she ever wants a writer to fulfill her, is already madly in love, if you will. No need to look far, just take me and Trigorin...Trigorin?

*(SORIN enters with NINA. He is in a wheelchair, she is pushing it)*

SORIN
So we are happy! We are merry today, finally? We are happy! Father and stepmother left for Boston, and we are free now for three entire days.

NINA
I am happy! I now belong to you.

SORIN
She is so pretty today.

ARKADINA
Well dressed, interesting... But let's not praise too much, or we will jinx her. Where is Trigorin?

NINA
He is fishing at the lake.

ARKADINA
How does he not get fed up with the fishing!

NINA
What is this?

ARKADINA
Maupassant, "On the Water," my dear. Well, then it goes on boring and untrue. My soul is restless. Tell me, what's with my son? Why is he so dull and stern? He spends entire days on the lake, I almost never see him.

MASHA
His heart is heavy. Please, read something from his play!

NINA
You want to? It's so boring!

MASHA
When he is reading something himself, his eyes
burn and his face turns pale. His voice has a
marvelous deep, sad and poetic manner.

DORN
Good night!

ARKADINA
Sorin!

SORIN
Huh?

ARKADINA
Are you asleep?

SORIN
Not at all.

ARKADINA
You are not taking care of yourself, and that's
not good, big brother.

SORIN
I would be happy to, but the doctor wouldn't
have anything then to do!

DORN
To be under doctor's care at age sixty.

SORIN
One wants to live even at sixty.

DORN
Well, take a sedative.

ARKADINA
I think it would be good for him to go somewhere to a spa.

DORN
Why not? He can go, or not go.

ARKADINA
Try to take this seriously.

DORN
There's nothing to take seriously.

MEDVEDENKO
He should quit smoking.

SORIN
Nonsense.

DORN
No, it's not nonsense. Alcohol and tobacco destroy your sense of self. After a cigar or a shot of whiskey you are no longer Sorin, but Sorin plus someone else; your sense of self is augmented and you relate to yourself as in a third person, as someone else.

SORIN
It's easy for you to expound on this. You have enjoyed your life, but I? I was a banker for twenty-eight years, but did not really live, did not experience anything, and finally here I am, and I think it's understandable, I really want to live some more. You are well fed and indifferent, and that's why you are philosophically inclined, but I want to live and that's why I drink whiskey at dinner and smoke cigars and that's all. That's all.

DORN
You need to take life seriously, but to go for treatments at sixty and feel sorry for yourself

that you did not enjoy your youth is, you'll forgive me, self-indulgent.

MASHA
It is time for breakfast, I suppose. *(Stamps foot)* My leg fell asleep... *(Exits)*

DORN
She will go and take two shots before breakfast.

SORIN
Poor child, she has no personal happiness.

DORN
Ridiculous.

SORIN
You talk like a well-fed man.

ARKADINA
Ah, can anything be more boring than this charming country boredom! Hot, quiet, no one is doing anything, everyone is philosophizing... I enjoy my time with you, friends, it's delightful, but to memorize lines in the dressing room is much more pleasant!

NINA
Yes! I understand you.

SORIN
Of course, it's better in the city. You sit in your office, the secretary does not let anyone in without an appointment, telephone, carriages outside and everything....

DORN
*(Singing)* "Pack up your troubles in your old kit bag, and smile, smile, smile..."

*(SHAMRAEV enters with POLINA)*

SHAMRAEV

Here they are. Good day! Very happy to see you in good health. My wife says that you are planning to go with her to the city today. Is that true?

ARKADINA

Yes, we are planning.

SHAMRAEV

Hmm, that's marvelous, but how are you going, my esteemed lady? Today they are hauling wheat, and all the hands are busy. So what horses are you taking, may I ask?

ARKADINA

What horses? Should I know, what horses?

SORIN

We have carriage horses.

SHAMRAEV

Carriage horses? But where will I get harnesses? Where will I get harnesses? This is outrageous! This is astonishing! Esteemed lady! Forgive me, I am in awe of your talent, I am ready to give ten years of my life for you, but I cannot give you horses!

ARKADINA

But if I must go! Sorin, do something!

SHAMRAEV

Esteemed lady! You do not understand what it takes to run a farm!

ARKADINA

And I have no wish to. I am leaving for New

York today. Hire a carriage for me in the village or I will walk to the station!

SHAMRAEV
In that case, I quit! Get yourself another estate manager! *(Storms out)*

ARKADINA
It's like this every summer, I am insulted here every summer! I will not set foot in this place again! *(Flounces out)*

SORIN
This is an insult! This is devil knows what! I am sick of this, finally. Order all the horses here immediately!

NINA
This is just incredible!

POLINA
What can I do? Put yourself in my place — what can I do?

SORIN
Let's go to my sister... We will all beg her not to leave.

NINA
Sit, sit, I will wheel you there...

SORIN
Don't you think? Insufferable person! Despot! But he will not quit, I will talk to him right now.

*(NINA wheels SORIN out)*

DORN
People are idiots. In reality, your husband should be fired, but instead, it will all end with

that old softy, Sorin, and his sister begging his forgiveness. You will see!

POLINA
He sent carriage horses to the field. And every day he makes such mistakes. If you knew, how this worries me! I am getting sick; you see, I am trembling... I cannot suffer his thoughtlessness. My dear Doctor, dear, precious, take me with you... Our time is running short, we are no longer young, so at least at the end of our lives to not hide, to not lie...

DORN
I am fifty-five, it is too late for me to change my life.

POLINA
I know, you are refusing me because beside me you have other women who are near and dear to you. You cannot take everyone with you. I understand. Forgive me.

DORN
*(Singing)* "I love you truly, truly, dear..."

POLINA
Truly?

*(NINA comes back with flowers)*

DORN
How is it in there?

NINA
Arkadina is crying, and Sorin is having an asthma attack.

DORN
I should give them both a sedative.

NINA
Please.

*(DORN exits)*

POLINA
What charming flowers! Give me these flowers!
I'll put them in water. *(Exits)*

NINA
How strange it is to see that a famous actress is
crying, and especially for such a silly reason. And
is it not strange that a famous writer, beloved
by the public, they are writing about him in
all the papers, selling his portraits, translating
him into foreign languages, and he is fishing all
day and is happy that he caught two minnows.
I thought that famous people are proud, unap-
proachable, that they despise the crowd and
with their fame and the sparkle of their name
they take their revenge on it, on the fact that
it puts breeding and wealth above all. But here
they are, crying, fishing, playing cards, laughing
and getting angry like everyone else..

*(CONSTANTINE enters)*

CONSTANTINE
Are you alone?

NINA
Yes, alone. Why?

CONSTANTINE
I was hateful enough to kill this seagull today. I
lay it at your feet.

NINA
What is wrong with you?

CONSTANTINE
Soon I will kill myself in the same manner.

NINA
I don't recognize you.

CONSTANTINE
Of course, after I stopped recognizing you.
You've changed, you no longer care about me,
your glance is cold, my very existence embarrasses you.

NINA
Lately you have been so prickly—so angry, you
confuse me, you try to talk to me with symbols.
Not real words or real feelings, but symbols.
And this seagull is apparently also some symbol,
but forgive me, I do not understand it... Maybe
I'm too stupid to understand you.

CONSTANTINE
You stopped caring from that evening when my
play failed so miserably. Women cannot forgive
failure. You know, I burned everything to the last
shred. God—if you could only see, only know
how unhappy I am! Your coldness is frightening, terrifying to me, as if I woke up as see that
this lake had dried up. You just said that you are
too stupid to understand me. But what is there
to understand? You did not like my play, you
despise my inspiration, you consider me medi-
ocre, worthless... I get it! And I agree! I have
no ability—but I do have ambition—I want to
have talent, I want to be good, but I'm not so
my ambition is just sucking my blood, like a
snake...

*(TRIGORIN enters, with a notebook)*

CONSTANTINE
Here comes the real talent, he is stepping out like Hamlet, and also with a book. "Words, words, words..." This sun has not yet approached you, but you are already smiling. I will not bother you anymore. *(Exits)*

TRIGORIN
*(Writing in his notebook)* She smokes cigarettes and drinks vodka... Always in black. The teacher loves her...

NINA
Hello, Trigorin!

TRIGORIN
Hello. And I suppose goodbye. The circumstances unexpectedly turned out that, it seems, we are leaving today. I doubt we will see each other again. That's a pity. It is not often that I meet young ladies, young and interesting ladies, and I've forgotten, and cannot imagine what one feels at eighteen or nineteen, and that's why in my novels and short stories young ladies are so very fake. I would like to spend an hour in your body, to understand what you are thinking and what you are generally about.

NINA
And how I would love to be in your place.

TRIGORIN
Why?

NINA
To understand, how a famous, talented writer

feels. How does fame feel? What do you feel when you are famous?

TRIGORIN
Well, nothing. I have never thought about it. So I suppose there are two choices: either you are exaggerating my fame, or fame feels like nothing.

NINA
And when you read about yourself in the papers?

TRIGORIN
It is pleasant when they praise me, but if they criticize me, I am in a foul mood for a couple of days.

NINA
Magical world! How I envy you, if you only knew! People have different lots. Some barely drag around their dull, invisible existence, all resembling each other, all unhappy; some, like you, for example, you are one in a million, were given an interesting, bright life full of meaning... You are happy...

TRIGORIN
Me? Hmm... Here you talk of fame, of happiness, of some bright interesting life, but to me all these nice words, forgive me, are like, well, oysters—which I never eat. You are very young and very kind.

NINA
Your life is wonderful!

## TRIGORIN

What is so especially wonderful about it? I need to go and write. Excuse me, I don't have time... You stepped on a sensitive spot, I guess, and so I am starting to get nervous and a little angry. Well, all right, let's discuss. Let's talk about my bright and wonderful life. With what shall we start? There are forced impressions, when a person thinks all day and all night, let's say, about the moon. And I have my own such moon. So day and night I am plagued by a thought: I must write, I must write, I must... As soon as I finish a novel for some reason I must write another one, then a third, then a fourth... I find I write incessantly, as if I were a mouse on a treadmill, going and going, and I cannot do it any other way. What is so bright and wonderful in this? Oh, what a crazy life! It's exhausting—it's draining—and it's everything. I am here with you, a little nervous, a little angry, yet every moment I remember, that an unfinished novel is waiting for me. I see a cloud, resembling a camel. I think, 'I need to mention in some story, that a cloud resembling a camel was floating by.' It smells of heliotrope. I tell myself, sickly sweet smell, widow's colors, must mention when describing a summer's eve. I catch myself on every phrase, on every word, and hurry to lock up these phrases and words in my literary closet. Maybe they will be useful! When I finish work, I run to the theater or go fishing. I should relax and forget, but no, shrapnel is already moving around in my head—new plotline, and it's pulling me to the desk, and I must write, I must write. And it is always like this, always, and I have no rest from myself, and I feel like I cannibalize my own life, that for the honey that I give to someone else I gather the pollen from my best flowers, I pick them and pull them and end up destroying their roots. Am I not crazy? Do my friends and relatives treat me like a sane healthy man? "What are you writing? What will you tell us about us?" It's all the same, it's all the same, and it seems to me that this attention, praises, admiration is all lies, they are lying to me like to a sick man, and I am sometimes afraid that they will sneak up on me, tie me up and take me to the asylum. And in those young years, my best years, in my youth, when I was starting out, my writing was one continuous torture. A minor writer, especially when he is unlucky in terms of publishing, feels himself clumsy, ill at ease, useless, superfluous, his nerves are taut, frayed; he is wandering around uncontrollably near those who are connected to literature and art, unrecognized, unnoticed by anyone, afraid to look in the eye directly and bravely, like a gambler who has no money. I rarely considered my reader, but when I did, I imagined him to be unfriendly, disdainful, and mistrustful. I was afraid of the public, it seemed fearsome to me, and each time a first printing was released, I imagined that men are hostile and women are coldly indifferent. It was awful. It was torture!

NINA

Please, allow me, but does not inspiration and
the very process of creating give you moments
of happiness?

TRIGORIN

Yes. When I write, it's... well... pleasant. I am
even content to read the proofs, but... as soon
as a work is published I cannot stand it, and
see that it is not as it was meant to be, it was
a mistake, I should have never written it, I am
discouraged, I feel disgust in my soul... And the
public reads, "Yes, lovely, talented... Lovely, but
nowhere near Hardy," or "Charming piece, but
Forrester's *Howard's End* is better". And that's
how it is until the grave, all lovely and talented,
lovely and talented, and that's all, and when I
die, all the acquaintances passing by my grave
will say, "Here lies Trigorin. He was a good
writer, but he was a worse writer than Tolstoy."

NINA

Please forgive me, but I refuse to understand
you. You are simply spoiled by success.

TRIGORIN

What success? I have never liked what I've
written. I have never liked myself. I don't like
myself like all writers. Worst of all is that I am in
some sort of a fog and often do not understand
what I am writing... I love this water, trees,
sky, I feel nature, it arouses passion in me, an
uncontrollable urge to write. But I am not just
a landscape painter. I love people, I feel that if
I am a writer, I must write about people, about

their suffering, about their success, about their future, about science, about human rights and so on and so forth, and I do write about everything, I am in a hurry, torn in all directions, so everyone is angry at me, so I run around like a fox chased by hounds, I see that life and science are forging ahead and are leaving me behind like a commuter who missed his train, and at the end I feel that I can only paint landscapes and in everything else I am a fraud, a fraud to the very marrow of my bones, to the center of my being.

NINA

You are overworked, and you have no time nor desire to comprehend your value. So you are dissatisfied with yourself, but to others you are great and wonderful! If I were such a writer as you I would give my whole life to the crowd, but would realize that its happiness is based only on reaching my heights, and it would carry me on its chariot.

TRIGORIN
On a chariot? What am I, Ben Hur?

NINA
For this happiness, to be a writer or an actress, I would suffer the lack of love from my near and dear ones... poverty, disappointment, I would live in an attic and eat only stale bread, I would suffer from dissatisfaction with myself, from realization of my own imperfections, but I would also demand fame, real, loud fame...

*(He takes hold of her face and kisses her)*

ARKADINA
*(Calling offstage)* Trigorin!

TRIGORIN
They are calling me, probably to pack. But I don't want to leave.

NINA
Do you see a house and a garden on the other bank?

TRIGORIN
Yes.

NINA
That is the manor of my late mother. I was born there. I spent my whole life near this lake and know every little island.

TRIGORIN
It is so perfect here! *(Notices the seagull)* What is that?

NINA
A seagull. Constantine shot it.

TRIGORIN
A beautiful bird. Really, I don't want to leave. I must convince Arkadina to remain.

NINA
What are you writing?

TRIGORIN
Just taking notes... A plot flickered... A plot for a short story... A young woman such as yourself lives on a lake since childhood, she loves the lake, like a seagull, and is happy and free like a seagull. But a man suddenly showed up and

having nothing better to do destroyed her like this seagull.

ARKADINA
*(Calling off-stage)* Trigorin, where are you?

TRIGORIN
Just a minute!

ARKADINA
*(Calling off-stage)* We are staying.

NINA
It's a dream!

*(Lights fade)*

END OF ACT TWO

# ACT III

*(Evening. On the veranda of the house, MASHA and TRIGORIN are sitting, a bottle between them. As lights come up, they each down the contents of a shot glass)*

MASHA
I am telling you this because you are a writer. You can use it. I am telling you honestly, if Constantine had seriously wounded himself, I don't know what I would have done, how I could live. But I am brave. So I decided, I will pull this love out of my heart, pull it out to the roots.

TRIGORIN
In what way?

MASHA
I am getting married.

*(Toasting, they do a shot)*

MASHA
To Medvedenko.

TRIGORIN
Wait—to the teacher?

MASHA
Yes.

TRIGORIN

I don't understand the need for this.

MASHA

It's a trap. To love hopelessly, to wait for something for years... It's a kind of a prison. But once I get married there will be no time for love, new concerns will overtake the old ones. And also, of course, it will be a change. Should we go again?

TRIGORIN

I think we've had enough.

MASHA

There you go! Don't look at me like that. (Pouring more shots) Women drink more often than you think. A few of us drink in the open, like me, but the majority drink in secret. Yes. And all vodka— no smell. To your future!

(They do a shot)

MASHA

You are a regular person, I am sorry to see you go.

TRIGORIN

I myself don't want to leave.

MASHA

So ask Dina to stay.

TRIGORIN

No, now she will not remain. Her son is behaving recklessly, tactlessly. He first shoots himself, and now, so I hear, plans to call me out for a duel. For a what? Really? He is sulking, sneering, preaching new forms of art and expression... You know, there is room for everyone, the new and the old—why all this pushing and shoving?

MASHA
Jealousy.

TRIGORIN
Jealousy?

MASHA
*(Pouring)* But that's none of my business.

*(They do a shot)*

MASHA
My teacher is not too smart, but he is a kind man and poor and loves me a lot.

*(TRIGORIN pours, they do a shot)*

Don't think badly of me. Send me your books, and definitely with your autograph. But don't write "Best regards" or something like that. Simply "To Masha, a poor relation, who lives who knows why." Good-bye!

*(MASHA starts to exit, sees NINA, goes back, gets the bottle, and leaves)*

NINA
*(Holding out her hands)* Even or odd?

TRIGORIN
Even.

NINA
No. I only have one bead in my hand. I wished, should I leave this place and become an actress —or not? I wish someone would advise me.

TRIGORIN
No one can advise about that.

NINA
We are parting... and will likely never meet again. I am asking you to accept this small token as a memento of me. I engraved the numbers of a couple of your verses... and on this side the name of your book, "Days and Nights."

TRIGORIN
How gracious! A lovely gift!

NINA
Remember me sometimes.

TRIGORIN
I will. I will remember, how you were on that beautiful day—do you remember?—a week ago, when you were in that light dress. We were talking... and there was a white seagull on the ground.

NINA
Yes, a seagull. We should not talk any more, someone is coming. I am begging you, give me just two minutes before you leave... *(Rushes out)*

*(Enter ARKADINA and SORIN, followed by YAKOV carrying luggage)*

ARKADINA
Stay home, old man. You, with your arthritis, should not be paying visits to people. Who just left? Nina?

TRIGORIN
Yes.

ARKADINA
I think I packed everything. I am exhausted.

TRIGORIN
"Days and Nights," page 121, verse 11 and 12.

YAKOV
Should I pack the fishing rods, too?

TRIGORIN
Yes, I will need them again. And give the books
to someone.

YAKOV
Your servant. *(Exits)*

TRIGORIN
Page 121, verses 11 and 12. And what's in those
verses? Are there any of my books here?

ARKADINA
In my brother's office, in the corner bookcase.

TRIGORIN
Corner bookcase... *(Exits towards the office)*

ARKADINA
Really, big brother, you should stay home...

SORIN
You are leaving, it is will be hard for me at home
without you.

ARKADINA
And what's in Montauk?

SORIN
Nothing special, but still. They will be laying the
cornerstone of the new courthouse and all that...
It would be nice to get away from this minnow
pond for an hour or two, because I am becoming
stale, like an old cigar. I ordered horses at one,
so we will leave at the same time.

**ARKADINA**

Well, live here, but don't be bored, and don't catch cold. Watch over my son. Care for him. Guide him. Once I leave, I will never know why Constantine tried to shoot himself. I think jealousy was the main reason, and the sooner I get Trigorin out of here, the better.

**SORIN**

How can I say? There were other reasons, too. It's understandable, he is a young man, smart, lives in the country, in the very depth of it in fact, without money of his own, without a reason for being, without a future. He is both ashamed and afraid of his indolence. I love him very much, and he is attached to me, but in the end he feels that he is superfluous in the house, that he is a hanger on, a poor relation. It's understandable, the young male ego...

**ARKADINA**

What a curse he is to me! Should he maybe enlist in the navy...

**SORIN**

I think, the best would be if you could... give him a little money. First of all, he needs to dress like a human being. He is dragging around in the same jacket for three years, walks around without a coat... And it would not be too harmful for him to revel a little... treat himself a bit... Go abroad, maybe... It is not too expensive.

**ARKADINA**

I suppose I can give something for a suit, but as for going abroad... No, at this time I cannot afford a suit, either. I have no money! No, I do not.

SORIN
So. I am sorry, my dear, don't be angry. I believe
you... You are a generous, noble woman.

ARKADINA
I don't have any money!

SORIN
If I had money, you understand, I would give
him some myself, but I have nothing, not a
penny. The estate manager takes my entire
pension and spends it on the house, the lawns,
the sheds, the boats, the cattle, the horses, the
orchards, the bees... and thus my money disap-
pears. Bees die, cow die, and they never give
me any horses...

ARKADINA
Yes, I have money, but I am an actress; my lifestyle and my wardrobe bankrupt me.

SORIN
You are kind, gentle... I respect you... Yes... I
am feeling something... Head is spinning. I am
unwell, and that's all.

ARKADINA
Sorin! Sorin, my dear... Help me! Help! He is
unwell!

(CONSTANTINE and MEDVEDENKO rush in)

SORIN
It's nothing, nothing, it passed, and that's all...

CONSTANTINE
Don't worry, mama, it's not dangerous. It happens
quite often with uncle these days. You, uncle,
need to lie down.

SORIN
Yes, a bit... But I will still go to Montauk... I
will rest and then I will go...

MEDVEDENKO
Here is a riddle. What walks in the morning on
four legs, in the afternoon on two, in the evening
on three...

SORIN
Exactly. And at night flat on my back. Thank you,
I can walk by myself...

*(With dignity, SORIN leaves the room)*

MEDVEDENKO
Well, you don't say!

ARKADINA
Oh, that scared me!

CONSTANTINE
It is unhealthy for him to live in the country. He
is pining. If you, mama, suddenly had a spell of
generosity and gave him a loan of one and a half
to two thousands, then he could live in the city
for an entire year.

ARKADINA
I have no money. I am an actress, not a banker.

CONSTANTINE
Mama, would you please change my bandage.

ARKADINA
The doctor is late.

CONSTANTINE
He promised to be here by ten, but it's already
noon.

ARKADINA

Sit. This looks like a turban. Yesterday some visitor was asking in the kitchen if you were rehearsing for Arabian Nights. It almost healed. There is almost nothing left. You will not do this... try this... this again, will you?

CONSTANTINE

*(lie)*

No, mama. That was a minute of insane desperation. It will not happen again. Your hands are magical. I remember, a long time ago, when you were still working at the Thalia Theatre at the Bowery, I was little then, there was fight in our yard, a laundry woman got beat up. Remember? She lost consciousness, and you kept visiting her, and brought her medicine, and helped take care of her kids. Do you remember? *Genuinly wants her to remember so she will treat him the same*

ARKADINA

No.

CONSTANTINE

Two ballerinas lived in the same building... They drank coffee with you... *she'll only remember something she finds exciting*

ARKADINA

That I remember.

CONSTANTINE *↑ (Be like them mom)*

They were very pious. Always complaining about being on their knees... Ohhhh. Lately, during these recent days, I have loved you dearly and *butter her up before trying to get info from her.* selflessly as I did in childhood. I have nothing left without you. Can I ask you something? Why, why are you with that man?

ARKADINA

You do not understand him, Constantine. He is

a man of character.

CONSTANTINE
Yet when they reported to him that I plan to
challenge him to a duel, his character did not
interfere with his cowardice. He is leaving. He
is shamefully running away! *show his mom her persf laws*

ARKADINA
What nonsense! I have asked him to leave.

CONSTANTINE
His character! You and I are almost fighting
because of him, and he is somewhere in the
guest room or in a garden, laughing at us... He
is encouraging Nina, convincing her once and
for all that he is a genius. *Doesn't actually want to fight - silly that they are*

ARKADINA
You enjoy telling me unpleasantries. I respect
this man, I care for this man, and I am asking you
to not speak ill of him in front of me.

CONSTANTINE
And I don't respect him. I don't care about him.
You want me to consider him a genius, but I'm
sorry, I do not know how to lie, like you, and his
writings make me sick. *Deflects writing insult from himself to Ark. Ver.*

ARKADINA
This is envy. People who are not talented, but are
pretentious, have nothing left to do but criticize
genuine talent.

CONSTANTINE
Genuine talent! I am more talented than all of
you, if this is what we are talking about! You,
mediocrities, took over art and consider only
that what you do as lawful and real, but you

suffocate and oppress everything else! I don't
accept you! I do not accept either you or him!

ARKADINA
Avant Garde dilettante!

CONSTANTINE
Go back to your charming theater and act in
pathetic, sentimental plays! *Again mocks theatre*
*abilities b/c she mocked*
*his*

ARKADINA
I have never acted in such plays. Just stop it!
You cannot even write a useless vaudeville!
Don't forget, you're just a petty nothing born in
Bridgeport, Connecticut!

CONSTANTINE
Selfish miser!

ARKADINA
Pretentious wannabe! Boring nonentity! Don't
cry. You shouldn't cry. There is no need... My
dear child, forgive me... Forgive your selfish
mother. Forgive me.

CONSTANTINE
If you only knew! I lost everything. She doesn't
love me, and I can no longer write... I've lost
all hope... *Fights b/c*
*he lacks*
*so much*
ARKADINA
Don't despair. It will pass. He will leave now,
and she will love you again. It's all right. We are
friends again.

CONSTANTINE
Yes, mama.

ARKADINA
Make up with him, too. No duels. There is no

need, right?

CONSTANTINE
All right... But, mama, please don't make me meet with him. It is too much for me, it's more than I can handle.. Here.. I will leave... And the doctor will take care of the bandage... *Needs emotional help too*

(CONSTANTINE exits as TRIGORIN enters reading his book)

TRIGORIN
Page 121... verses 11 and 12... Here... "If you ever have a need of my life, then come and take it."

ARKADINA
Soon they will saddle the horses.

TRIGORIN
If you ever have a need of my life, then come and take it.

ARKADINA
I hope you are all packed?

TRIGORIN
Let's stay another day! Let's stay!

ARKADINA
My dear, I know what is holding you here. But control yourself. You are a little drunk—sober up.

TRIGORIN
Then you should also be sober, be smart, be sensible, I beg of you, look at all of this as a true friend... You are capable of sacrifice... Be my friend, let me go...

**ARKADINA**
You are so infatuated?

**TRIGORIN**
I am compelled to be with her! Maybe that is
exactly what I need.

**ARKADINA**
Love of a little provincial girl?

**TRIGORIN**
Sometimes people are sleepwalking, so I am
talking to you, but it is as if I am asleep and see
her in my dreams. I am in the thrall of sweet,
wonderful dreams. Let me go...

**ARKADINA**
No, no... I am not ordinary, you cannot speak
to me like this... Don't torment me, Trigorin...
You're scaring me...

**TRIGORIN**
If you wanted to, you could be extraordinary.
Young love, charming, poetic, sweeping us into
the world of dreams—it alone can bring happiness on earth! I have never yet felt such love... I
had no time in my youth, I was so busy knocking
on the doors of editors, I fought with constant
poverty... And now she is here, and this love, it
finally came to me, it beckons me... How can I
run from it?

**ARKADINA**
You have lost your mind!

**TRIGORIN**
So what.

**ARKADINA**
You have all conspired today to torment me.

**TRIGORIN**
She does not understand! She refuses to understand!

**ARKADINA**
Am I so old and hideous that you can talk to me about other women without embarrassment? Oh, you have gone mad! My wonderful, my amazing… You are the last page in my life story! My joy, my pride, my bliss.. If you leave me even for an hour, I will not survive, I will lose my mind, my incredible, my marvelous, my genius, my ruler…

**TRIGORIN**
Someone may come in.

**ARKADINA**
Let them, I am not ashamed of my love for you. My treasure, so reckless, you want to lose your head, but I don't want you to, I won't let you… You are mine…mine… This forehead is mine, these eyes are mine, and this wonderful silky hair is also mine… You are all mine. You are so talented, smart, the best of today's writers, you are literature's only hope… You have so much sincerity, honesty, freshness, healthy and true humor… With one pass of the pen you convey the most important image for a character or a landscape, your people are alive. Oh, I cannot read your works without excitement! So much excitement. You think I lie to you? That I flatter you? Well, look into my eyes. Put your hand on my skin. Feel the beat of my heart. Do I seem

to be a liar? See, I alone know how to appreci-
ate you, I alone tell you the truth my dear, my
wonderful one. You will come with me? Yes?
You will not abandon me?

TRIGORIN
I have no will of my own. I have never had a will
of my own. I am vague... always compliant—
how can women like this? Take me, take me away,
but do not let me out of your sight...

ARKADINA
Yes. You are mine. Actually, if you wish, you can
stay. I will leave alone, and then you can join me
in a week. Really, what's the hurry?

TRIGORIN
No, of course not, let's leave together.

ARKADINA
As you wish. Together is fine. Penny for your
thoughts?

TRIGORIN
I heard a nice expression this morning, "a maiden
grove..." It will be useful. So, let's go? Again
wagons, stations, cafeterias, beef steaks, conver-
sations...

(Enter SHAMRAEV and POLINA, followed by
YAKOV carrying boxes)

SHAMRAEV
I must regretfully inform you that the carriage
is ready. It is time, my esteemed one, to leave
for the station; the train arrives at five after two.
Please do me a favor, and find out where the
actor Frederick Freeman Potter is. Is he alive?
Is he well? We used to drink together... There's

no rush, my esteemed one, you still have five minutes. Once he played a villain in a melodrama, and when they were suddenly discovered, the line was "I am trapped," but Potter said "I am rapped!" Rapped!

POLINA
Here are some plums for your journey. They are very sweet. Maybe you will want a treat.

ARKADINA
You are very kind, Polina, dear.

POLINA
Farewell, my dear! If something was amiss, please forgive me.

ARKADINA
Everything was good, everything was good. There is no need to cry.

POLINA
Our time runs short!

SORIN
Sister, it's time, we should not be late, finally. I am going to board.

MEDVEDENKO
And I will walk to the station, to see you off. Right away...

ARKADINA
Good bye, my dears. If we are all healthy and well, we will meet again next summer. Do not forget me.

SHAMRAEV
Don't forget to write! Farewell, Trigorin!

ARKADINA

Where is Constantine? Tell him, that I am leaving. We need to say good bye. Well, don't speak ill of me.

*(She exits, he starts after her and then NINA enters)*

TRIGORIN

I forgot my notebook. I think it's on the terrace. We are leaving...

NINA

I know that we will meet again. Trigorin, I have made my decision, and the die is cast, I am going on the stage. Tomorrow I will no longer be here, I am leaving my father, leaving everything, starting a new life... I am leaving like you, I am going to New York. We will meet there.

TRIGORIN

Let me know as soon as you arrive. The Endicott Hotel... I am in a rush...

NINA

Just one more minute.

TRIGORIN

You are so beautiful, I will see you soon; these marvelous eyes, this inexpressibly wonderful smile, the expression of poetic innocence ...

*(They kiss. Lights fade)*

## END OF ACT THREE

# ACT IV

*(Night in CONSTANTINE's study. An autumnal storm lashes the windows)*

MASHA
Constantine! Constantine! No one's here. His uncle is asking every minute, where is Constantine... He can't live without him...

MEDVEDENKO
He is afraid of loneliness. What dreadful weather! The second day of rain.

MASHA
There are huge waves on the lake.

MEDVEDENKO
We should tell Yakov to break apart that folly in the garden. It sits there naked, ugly, like a skeleton, bending in the wind. Yesterday evening when I was passing by, I thought someone was crying in there...

MEDVEDENKO
Masha, let's go home!

MASHA
I will be spending the night here.

MEDVEDENKO
Masha, let's go! The baby is probably hungry.

MASHA
Your mother will feed him.

MEDVEDENKO
I feel so sorry for him. It's already his third night
without his mother.

MASHA
You have become dull. Before you at least used
to philosophize, and now it's just baby, go home,
baby, go home—and that's all I hear from you.

MEDVEDENKO
Let's go, Masha!

MASHA
Go yourself.

MEDVEDENKO
Your father will not give me a horse.

MASHA
He will. Ask, and he will.

MEDVEDENKO
I guess I will ask. So, will you come home tomorrow?

(POLINA enters with bedding)

MASHA
All right, tomorrow. Pest... What is this for,
mama?

POLINA
Sorin asked to put his bedding in Constantine's
study. Old man is like an infant..

MEDVEDENKO
So I am leaving. Good bye, Masha. Good bye, mother.

POLINA
Eh! Just go.

*(CONSTANTINE enters)*

MEDVEDENKO
Good bye, Constantine.

POLINA
Who could have ever guessed that you would turn into a real writer. And now, thank God, you get money sent from magazines. And you became so handsome. Dear Constantine, honey, be gentler with my Masha!

MASHA
Leave him alone, mama.

POLINA
She is so sweet. A woman, Constantine, does not need anything else, just a gentle look. I know that from my own experience.

*(CONSTANTINE exits)*

MASHA
Now you have made him mad. Did you need to bother him like that?!

POLINA
I feel sorry for you, Masha, my dear.

MASHA
Like I need that!

POLINA
My heart aches for of you. I see everything, I

understand everything.

MASHA
This is all stupidity. Unrequited love is just the stuff of romances. It's nonsense. One just can't keep waiting. Once love planted itself in the heart, if not returned, it must be pulled out. The school promised to transfer my husband to another county. Once we move there, I will forget everything, pull it out by the roots...

*(The strains of a piano)*

POLINA
Constantine is playing. He must be pining.

MASHA
The main thing, mama, is not to see. I just wish they would transfer my husband, and then, believe me, I will forget within a month. This is all nonsense.

*(Enter MEDVEDENKO and, separately, CONSTANTINE and DORN)*

MEDVEDENKO
I have six mouths to feed in my house now. And a loaf of bread costs nearly 3 cents...

DORN
So you keep hustling.

MEDVEDENKO
It's easy for you to laugh. You have plenty of money.

DORN
Money? During thirty years of practice, my friend, restless work when I did not belong to myself day or night, I managed to save only a few

thousand, and even that I recently spent abroad. I have nothing.

MASHA
Are you still here?

MEDVEDENKO
How will I go? Your father will not five me a horse!

MASHA
I wish I'd never set eyes on him!

DORN
But you have had so many changes! You turned a parlor into an office.

MASHA
It is more convenient for Constantine to work here. He can just go out to the garden and think.

*(Enter SORIN)*

SORIN
Where is my sister?

DORN
She went to the station to meet Trigorin. She will be back soon.

SORIN
If you felt it necessary to call my sister here I must be seriously ill. Here is the story: I am seriously ill, and he won't give me any medicine. And that's all.

DORN
What do you want? A sedative? Soda? Quinine?

SORIN
Now he starts prescribing. Is that bedding for me?

POLINA
For you, Sorin, dear.

SORIN
I thank you.

DORN
*(Singing)* "After the ball is over, after the break of day..."

SORIN
I want to give Constantine a plot for a novel. It must be called "The man who wanted." In my youth I wanted to become a writer—and did not become one; I wanted to speak eloquently—I spoke ridiculously; I wanted to get married—I did not get married; I always wanted to live in the city—and here I am, dying in the country, and that's all.

DORN
You wanted to run a bank, and you did.

SORIN
I never aimed for it. It just happened.

DORN
To express dissatisfaction with your life at age sixty-two, you must agree, is petty.

SORIN
You are so stubborn. Please understand, I want to live!

DORN
Well, too bad. The laws of nature dictate that every life must have an end.

SORIN
You talk like a well fed person. You are well fed,

and so are indifferent to life, you don't care. But even you will fear dying.

DORN
The fear of death is an animal fear. You have to ignore it. Only those who believe in eternal life are consciously fearing death, because they fear their sins. But you are first of all a nonbeliever, and second, what sins do you have? You served the bank, faithfully, for twenty-five years, and that's all.

SORIN
Twenty-eight...And that's all!

DORN
We are interrupting Constantine's work.

CONSTANTINE
It's no bother.

MEDVEDENKO
May I ask, doctor, what foreign city did you like the most?

DORN
Genoa.

CONSTANTINE
Why Genoa?

DORN
It has a superb night life. When you leave your hotel in the evening, the whole street is full of people. You simply exist in the crowd without any purpose, live with it, blend with it physically, psychically, and start believing in the one soul in the world—like that one that Nina acted in your play. By the way, where is Nina these

days? Where is she and how is she?

CONSTANTINE
I suppose she is well.

DORN
I heard she has been leading an unusual life. Is she?

CONSTANTINE
It is a long story, doctor.

DORN
So shorten it.

CONSTANTINE
She ran away from home and became Trigorin's... paramour. Did you know this?

DORN
Yes.

CONSTANTINE
They had a baby. The baby died. Trigorin fell out of love with her and returned to... his previous attachments... as would have been expected. Well, in truth, he never actually left... his previous attachments... but due to his lack of character, managed both here and there. As I could understand from what I learned, Nina's personal life did not work out at all.

DORN
And the stage?

CONSTANTINE
Much worse. She made her debut in the outskirts of Boston, at a summer theater, then she moved further out. Smaller and smaller theatres... At that time I was keeping up with her and follow-

ing her career. She was getting leading parts, but acted clumsily, without charm. There were moments when she screamed capably, died competently, but they were mere moments.

DORN
So she has some talent after all?

CONSTANTINE
It was hard to tell. Maybe, yes. I wanted to see her, but she did not want to see me. I understood her mood and did not insist on a meeting. What else can I tell you? Later, after I'd already returned home, I received some letters from her. The letters were friendly, warm, interesting; she didn't complain, but I felt that she was deeply unhappy; each line was a painful, frayed nerve. And her imagination was a bit fanciful. She signed her letters as "Seagull." She kept repeating that she is a seagull. And now she is here.

DORN
What do you mean, here?

CONSTANTINE
Here. In town, at an inn. She has been there for five days already. I went to try to see her, and Masha went, but she is not accepting visitors. Medvedenko said that yesterday after dinner her saw her in the field, two miles from here.

MEDVEDENKO
Yes, I saw her. She was walking in that direction, toward town. I bowed, asked why she does not visit us. She said that she will.

CONSTANTINE
She won't. Her father and stepmother don't want

to know her. They put guards everywhere to not even let her get near the manor house. How easy it is, in theory, doctor, and how difficult it is in real life!

SORIN
She was a lovely young lady.

DORN
What?

SORIN
I am saying, she was a lovely young lady. I think I was even in love with her at one point. And that's all.

DORN
Dirty old man.

POLINA
I think they have arrived from the station...

CONSTANTINE
Yes, I hear my mother.

SHAMRAEV
We are getting older, drying up in the wind, and you, esteemed one, are still youthful... Colorful clothes, lively, elegant...

ARKADINA
You again want to jinx me, you backward man!

TRIGORIN
Hello, Sorin! Why is that you are still sick? That's no good! Masha!

MASHA
You recognized me.

TRIGORIN
Are you married?

MASHA
For a long time.

TRIGORIN
Happily?

MASHA
Ehh.

ARKADINA
Trigorin brought magazine with your new short story.

CONSTANTINE
Thank you, you are very kind.

TRIGORIN
Your admirers send their greetings. They are very interested in you in New York and in Boston, everyone is asking me about you. They are wondering, what is he like, how old, is he brunet or blond. For some reason everyone thinks that you are not young. And no one knows your real name, as you only publish under a pseudonym. You are mysterious, like the Man in the Iron Mask.

CONSTANTINE
Are you here for long?

TRIGORIN
No, I am thinking of leaving for New York tomorrow. I need to. I am in a hurry to finish a novel, and I also promised to come up with something for a journal. In other words, same old story. The weather here did not greet me

gently. The wind is fierce. But tomorrow morning, if it quiets down, I'd like to go fishing. By
the way, we need to examine the garden and
that spot, where—you remember—your play was
performed. I have an idea...

MASHA
Papa, please let my husband take a horse! He
needs to go home.

SHAMRAEV
Horse... home... You have seen yourself, they
just came from the station. It's not possible to
make them go again.

MASHA
Good god—there are other horses... To deal
with you...

MEDVEDENKO
I will walk, Masha, really...

POLINA
To walk in such weather...

MEDVEDENKO
It's only six miles. Good bye, Mother. Good bye.
I will not bother anyone! Good bye.

SHAMRAEV
The walk will do him good.

POLINA
Please, ladies and gentlemen. Supper is nearly
ready.

ARKADINA
During these long fall evenings, we play bingo
here. Look, here's that old set of mother's we

used to pay with when we were children. Let's play a game before supper!

CONSTANTINE
He read his own novel, but did not even cut the pages of mine.

ARKADINA
What about you, Constantine?

CONSTANTINE
Forgive me, I don't really want to... I am going for a walk. *(Exits)*

ARKADINA
The bet is a penny. Put one up for me, doctor.

DORN
*A votre service.*

MASHA
Everyone placed their bets? I am starting. Twenty-two!

ARKADINA
Yes.

MASHA
Three!

DORN
Here.

MASHA
Everyone put three down? Eight! 81! 10!

SHAMRAEV
Slow down.

ARKADINA
How they received me in Philadelphia, dear

Lord, my head is still spinning!

MASHA
Thirty-four!

ARKADINA
The students from the college organized a standing ovation.. Three baskets of flowers, two wreaths, and...

SHAMRAEV
Yes, that is something...

MASHA
Fifty!

DORN
Exactly Fifty?

ARKADINA
I wore an amazing costume... Say what you will, but I know how to wear a dress.

POLINA
Constantine is suffering, poor boy.

SHAMRAEV
They are criticizing him a lot in the papers.

MASHA
Seventy-seven!

ARKADINA
Who cares about the critics?

TRIGORIN
He is unlucky. He just cannot find his real voice. There is something strange, unidentifiable, sometimes resembling ravings. No living faces or forms.

MASHA
Eleven!

ARKADINA
Sorin, are you bored? He is asleep.

DORN
The banker is asleep.

MASHA
Seven! Ninety!

TRIGORIN
If I lived in such a manor house, by the lake, would I have started writing? I would conquer this passion and would do nothing but fish.

MASHA
Twenty-eight!

TRIGORIN
It is such bliss to catch a perch or a bass!

DORN
But I believe in Constantine. There is something there! There is something! He thinks in images, his stories are colorful, bright, and I feel them keenly. It's just a pity that he has no set goals. He makes an impression, and that's all, but I suppose you cannot go far with mere impressions. Arkadina, are you proud of your son's career?

ARKADINA
If you can imagine, I have not yet read anything. I just haven't had time.

MASHA
Twenty-six!

SHAMRAEV
Trigorin, we still have something of yours.

TRIGORIN
What?

SHAMRAEV
One time Constantine shot a seagull, and you told me to stuff it.

TRIGORIN
I do not remember. I do not remember.

MASHA
Sixty-six! One!

*(CONSTANTINE re-enters)*

CONSTANTINE
It's so dark! I don't understand why I am so restless.

MASHA
Eighty-eight!

TRIGORIN
I have a match, ladies and gentlemen.

ARKADINA
Bravo! Bravo!

SHAMRAEV
Bravo!

ARKADINA
This man is always lucky, and everywhere he is lucky. And now let's go eat. Our renowned guest has not yet eaten today. We will continue after supper. Constantine, leave your writings and let's go eat.

CONSTANTINE

I don't want to, mother, I'm not hungry.

ARKADINA

As you wish. Sorin, supper! I will tell you about the reception in Philadelphia...

*(Exit all save CONSTANTINE)*

CONSTANTINE

I used to talk about the new forms so much, but now I feel that I am slipping into a routine. "The sign on the fence stated... Pale face, framed by dark hair..." Stated, framed... This is inept. I will start with the hero being awoken by the rain, and the rest is gone. The description of the moonlight evening is long and rarefied. Trigorin developed his tricks, it's easy for him... He has the neck of a broken bottle sparkling on the dam and the shadow of the miller wheel is darkening—and the moonlit night is ready, and I have flickering light, and quiet sparkling of the stars, and faraway piano notes, melting in the quiet fragrant air... It's torturous. Yes, I am more and more coming to the conclusion that the issue is not old and new forms, but in the person writing without regard for the forms, writing because it freely flows from his soul.

*(NINA enters, drenched)*

CONSTANTINE

What's that? I can't see anything... Someone's here? Who is here? Nina! Nina! Nina! Nina! It's you... you... It's like I felt it, my soul was aching greatly all day. Oh, my love, my precious, you came! Let's not cry, let's not.

NINA
Someone else is here.

CONSTANTINE
There is no one.

NINA
Lock the doors, or they will come in.

CONSTANTINE
No one will come in.

NINA
I know that your mother is here. Lock the doors.

CONSTANTINE
There is no lock. Don't worry, no one will come
in.

NINA
Let me look at you. It's warm here, nice... This
used to be just a parlor. Did I change a lot?

CONSTANTINE
Yes. You are thinner, and your eyes are bigger.
Nina, it's so strange that I am seeing you. Why
would you not admit me when I came to call?
Why did you not visit me until now? I know,
you have been living in town for almost a week.
I have been coming to your house several times
a day, I threw pebbles at your window...

NINA
I was afraid that you hate me. I have nightmares
every night, that you are looking at me and
looking through me. If you only knew! Since
my arrival I have been walking around here, by
the lake. I was near your house many times, but
couldn't bring myself to enter. Let's sit down.

Let's sit down and talk, talk. It's so nice here, so warm and cozy. Do you hear the wind? Turgenev has this one quote, "It is blissful to be the one, who on such a night sits under his own roof, who has a warm corner." I am a seagull. No, not this. What was I talking about? Yes, Turgenev... "And may God help all the homeless wanderers." It's nothing...

CONSTANTINE
Nina, there you are again... Nina!

NINA
It's nothing, I feel better now. I have finally cried—and I have not cried in two years. Yesterday late evening I went to the garden, to see if the space for our theatre is still the same. And it is. It's just the same. I cried for the first time in two years, and my heart grew lighter, and my soul became clearer. You are a writer, I am an actress... We are in a whirlpool... I used to live happily like a child—you wake up in the morning and sing; I loved you, I dreamed about fame, and now. Tomorrow early in the morning I need to go to Bridgeport, third-class, and in Bridgeport I will be bothered by the advances of shopowners and factory workers and try to avoid the circus...

CONSTANTINE
Bridgeport?

NINA
I have an engagement for the entire winter. It's time to go.

CONSTANTINE
Nina, I cursed you, I hated you, I tore up your

letters and photos, but I realized each moment
that my soul is forever tied to you. I have no
power to stop loving you, Nina. Since I lost you
and started publishing, life became unendur-
able. I am suffering. My youth just ended, and
I feel as if I have been living in this world for
nine hundred years. My soul is calling to you,
I am kissing the ground you walked on, everywhere I look I imagine your face, your smile,
which lit up the best years of my life…

NINA
Why are you talking like this?

CONSTANTINE
I am *lonely*. No one warms me with their affec-
tions, I am cold like in a subterranean cave, and
everything that I write is dry, harsh, cold. Stay
here, Nina, I am begging you, or let me leave
with you! Nina, why, for God's sake, Nina…

NINA
I have to go. Don't see me off, I will see myself
out. Give me some water…

CONSTANTINE
Where are you going now?

NINA
To Montauk. Your mother is here?

CONSTANTINE
Yes… Uncle was unwell on Thursday, so we sent
her a telegram to get here.

NINA
Why do you say, that you are kissing the ground
I walked on? I should be shot. I am so tired!

I am a seagull... No, not that. I am an actress. Yes! And he is here... That's all right, it doesn't matter... Yes... He does not believe in theater, he laughed at my dreams, he laughed and little by little I also stopped believing and it became hard... And then there were the trials of love, and then jealousy, and constant fear for my little one... I became petty, my thoughts trivial and small, I acted without meaning... I did not know what to do with my hands, I could not stand on the stage, I could not control my voice. You do not understand what that feels like, when you know that you are acting badly. I am a seagull. No, not that.... Do you remember when you shot a seagull? A man casually showed up and saw something beautiful and, having nothing better to do, destroyed it... A plot for a short story... What was I talking about? I am talking about the stage. Now I am not like that... I am a real actress now, I act with my entire being, I act with pleasure, with exultation, I am drunk from the stage and the words and I feel marvelous. And now, while I live here, I walk, I walk and think, think and feel how my emotional strength increases every day. I now know, I understand, Constantine, that in our business it does not matter, whether we act or write, the most important thing is not fame, not glory, not that of which I dreamed, but the ability to hope. To keep on. To carry your cross and have faith. I have faith, and so I do not hurt as much, and when I think of my calling, I am not afraid of life.

**CONSTANTINE**
You found your path in life, you know where you are going, but I am still groping in the chaos of images and dreams, without knowing who needs it and why. I have no faith, and I do not know what my calling is.

**NINA**
Shh... I am going. Good bye. When I become a famous actress, you must come see me. You promise? But now... It's late. I am barely standing up... I am starving, I need to eat...

**CONSTANTINE**
Stay, I will feed you supper.

**NINA**
No, no... Don't see me off, I will see myself out... So, she brought him with her? Well, who cares. When you see Trigorin, don't tell him anything. I love him. I love him even more than before... A plot for a short story... I love him, love him passionately, to distraction. It was nice before, Constantine! Remember? It was such a bright, clear, clean, warm life, such feelings—feeling that were like tender, delicate flowers... Remember? "People, lions, eagles and quails, horned stags, geese, spiders, silent fish inhabiting the waters, stars of the sea and those invisible to the naked eye, in other words, all lives, all lives, all lives, having completed their sad circle, went out... Already thousands of centuries since the earth does not contain any living beings, and this poor moon lights its lamp in vain. Cranes no longer wake crying in the meadows, and the beetles are not heard in the linden groves..."

*(NINA leaves. CONSTANTINE watches her go)*

CONSTANTINE
It would not be good if someone were to see her in the garden and then tell mother. It could upset mother...

*(DORN enters followed by ARKADINA, TRIGORIN, POLINA, SHAMRAEV)*

DORN
What were you saying?

CONSTANTINE
Nothing important.

*(CONSTANTINE exits)*

DORN
Strange...

ARKADINA
Here's the red wine and beer for Trigorin. We will play and drink. Let's sit down, ladies and gentlemen.

POLINA
Bring tea at once, too.

SHAMRAEV
Here is the thing about which I was telling you the other day. Your order.

TRIGORIN
I don't remember! I don't remember!

*(Sound of a shotgun)*

ARKADINA
What was that?

DORN

Nothing. Something must have exploded in my medical bag. Don't worry. That's all it was. A jar of ether must have exploded.

*(DORN exits—there is a pause and then conversation starts again)*

ARKADINA

Ugh, it frightened me. It reminded me how... Everything went dark before my eyes...

*(DORN returns)*

DORN

*(To TRIGORIN)* Two months ago there was an article published... a letter from Russia, and I wanted to ask you, by the way... because I am very interested in this issue... Take Arkadina away somewhere. What I mean is, Constantine shot himself...

*(Lights fade)*

## END OF PLAY

# CFP—CONCEPT FOR PRODUCTION: "THE SEAGULL"

*When we first began working together, Scenic Designer Jeromy Hopgood sent me a set of excellent questions regarding the show we were working on. Since then, I have adopted those questions into my standard Concept For Production forms. Below is the CFP for our 2017 production of The Seagull.*

## 1. In what time period do you see this production staged?

The time is 1896-1898 (give or take some years, I'm not planning on showing any newspapers).

While the play itself is, of course, based in Russia, I plan to move it all to an estate in New England—upstate New York or CT. I want to shift away from the "Russian" aspects of the play that the audience will find distancing or challenging.

It's mainly a summer play: evenings on the lawn and soft, breezy fabrics. Until Act IV—which is a stormy spring night—prior to the trees budding, when the world is just muddy.

## 2. What is the significance of this time period to the production?

The turn of the 20th century was a general time of major change in artistic styles. The younger artists were crying for innovation, startling honesty, a break from sentimentality. And I love using the Expressionists palettes.

**3. What is the central theme of this production? (What theme do you most want communicated?)**

Is the "artistic temperament" an insurmountable hurdle to happiness?

**4. Give 3 adjectives that best describe the overall feel this production should have.**

Funny: The Seagull has great wit and humor in its dialogue—it's a true comedy—although often bitter.

Dramatic: there is melodrama in the show, shocking behavior, and a great deal of larger-than-life reactions— and that's not a bad thing—at times it's hilariously funny as we watch our characters behave badly or ridiculously, at times it's almost embarrassing for the same reasons, and at times it's quite painful. These characters have larger-than-life egos and passions—and often consider themselves above the plain on which mere mortals dwell—and a world that enjoys Lifestyles of the Rich and Famous enjoys watching these entitled and spoiled lovers.

Unexpected: Chekhov is known for long dramatic plays with drab costumes and people who never make it to Moscow. Let's surprise them. Let's make it fast, two hours in length, a delightfully breezy... until it's not.

**5. Are there specific technical needs that you feel you must have in order to have a successful production? (In the areas of scenery, lighting, costumes, sound, props, and/or effects)**

At this time, I'm not seeing anything out of the

ordinary. But that may change a bit as the text grows.

I like for Acts 1-3 to have a summer, bleached out palette for the costumes—with deeper and more earthy colors for Act IV—if this is possible.

**Arkadina**: 'Dina: 45, stage actress diva. Undeniably talented, undeniably charismatic—while she is always conscious of the image she projects, it comes from a real place of knowing that image is her meal ticket. She is casually narcissistic and yet casually loving. Her deepest fear is being alone and unloved... but if she ends up that way, she won't be forgotten or poor.

**Sorin**: Her older brother, 60, a wealthy retired banker. Made a lot of money in his career, but nothing out of the ordinary. By usual standards, he's loaded— by the standards of the world he existed in during his working years, he's broke. Never married, no children, many regrets. Loves his sister and her son, whom he had a large part in raising. Unlike so many of the people he's not an artist, not good at expressing himself—but very good at being liked in a group.

**Trigorin**: Her lover: 35. A talented writer who's rather surprised at his own success. A man comfortable with his thoughts and in his head, less at home in groups or being asked to talk about his own work. While he's ambitious, he's not confident in his abilities. Loves Arkadina for her clarity, her fundamental knowledge of herself and her world—doesn't mean he always likes her.

**Constantine**: Her son. 25. A young man raised in relative comfort but not allowed any agency. His presence in his mother's world dates her and often embarrasses her—but while wanting to be a part of that world, he also scorns it and considers it shallow and inconsequential. Has the black-and-white thinking of many young artists – different is good, classic is useless, no one has ever had the thoughts he has. Loves hard, but without understanding.

**Nina**: The perfect blank canvas: everyone sees in her what they want to see. She's young, sheltered so emotionally young, she's been both betrayed and practically abandoned by her father, but has accepted it and has not fought her captivity. Everyone around her sees what they want in her: to Constantine she is a goddess and a muse, to Trigorin she is vitality, honesty, youth and creativity, to Arkandina she is a threat. Not until she goes through proverbial hell does she discover who she is: a not overly talented actress.

**Dr. Dorn**: Local doctor, friend of the Sorin family. Well-to-do but not loaded. A real lover (not a fighter) who has spent most of his life being the suave gentlemen dining and dancing women and never getting close. Now he's 55 and alone... and feeling it.

**Masha**: Grew up on Sorin's estate, daughter of the caretaker and housekeeper. In love with Constantine, but also in love because she's knows it's impossible. Literally "settles" for her life throughout.

**Polina**: Masha's mother, married to Shamraev. Similar to Masha in almost every way—but found a way to keep her dreams alive through hopes for her daughter's future and through a random affair with Dr. Dorn (who, in her youth, was her Constantine.)

**Shamraev**: The caretaker of Sorin's estate. As "boss" of the servants, he thinks highly of his position— he has many opinions, and in his daily life, the servants are forced to hear them: has a harder time with his bosses. Proud of his position and his family. Honestly thinks he's living the good life.

**Medvedev**: The local schoolteacher, in love with Masha. So similar to her father with an added quality of whiney Marxism.

**Yakov**: 25. Works on the estate. Basically a sight gag—every time he goes by he's being sent to work on something or carrying boxes and bags and luggage.

# ABOUT THE PLAYWRIGHT

Anton Chekhov was born on January 29, 1860, in Taganrog in southern Russia on the Azov Sea. After graduating from high school with every honor, he entered the University of Moscow as a student of medicine, and threw himself headlong into a double life of student and author, in the attempt to help his struggling family.

His first story appeared in a Moscow paper in 1880. During his student years, he poured forth a succession of short stories and sketches of Russian life with incredible rapidity. He wrote during every spare minute, in crowded rooms where there was "no light and less air," and never spent more than a day on any one story.

His audience demanded laughter above all things, and, with his deep sense of the ridiculous, Chekhov was happy to oblige. His stories, though often based on themes profoundly tragic, are penetrated by the light and subtle satire that won him his reputation as a great humorist. But though there was always a smile on his lips, it was a tender one, and his sympathy with suffering often brought his laughter near to tears.

From the late 1890s onward, Chekhov collaborated with Constantin Stanislavski and the Moscow Art Theater on productions of his plays, including his masterpieces The Seagull (1895), Uncle Vanya (1897), The Three Sisters (1901) and The Cherry Orchard (1904).

Chekhov died of tuberculosis on July 15, 1904, in Badenweiler, Germany.

# ABOUT THE TRANSLATOR

Alexandra LaCombe comes by her love of Anton Chekhov honestly, having studied his writings in school back in the USSR, and later on at the University of Michigan. The complete works of Chekhov was one of the prized items in Alexandra's family's possessions brought along to the US.

Alexandra is a fervent reader in Russian, English, and French, and counts David Blixt among her favorite authors. She is also devoted to live theater, primarily as a spectator. Alexandra's short stories were published over the years in the Russian language press in the US, but this is her first venture into translation.

Alexandra is working toward a life goal of being able to say that she is a "former attorney"

# ABOUT THE ADAPTOR

The Artistic Director of the Michigan Shakespeare Festival since 2010, Janice L Blixt has become the state's most award-winning director/producer. In addition to bold stagings of Shakespeare from *Hamlet* to *Measure For Measure*, Blixt has challenged herself to produce new versions of classic stories, including adaptations of Chekhov's *The Seagull* and Aphra Behn's *The Rover*, Karen Tarjan's adaptation of Michael Shaara's novel *The Killer Angels*, and award-winning productions of Wilde and Shaw.

A working director in Chicago for the past fifteen years, Blixt has helmed *Julius Caesar, Macbeth, Twelfth Night, The Taming of the Shrew, A Midsummer Night's Dream*, and the critically heralded *Titus Andronicus*. She has also been the vocal director and text coach for *Othello, Edward III*, and *Hamlet*. She is a co-founder and Executive Director of A Crew of Patches Theatre Company, a professional Shakespearean repertory company in Chicago that produces full-length Shakespeare plays for high schools. She directed *Captain Blood* and *Women In Jeopardy* at First Folio and teaches text analysis and folio technique for professional actors and in colleges and is still, when there's time, a working actor.

A graduate of the Hilberry Theater's MFA program, Blixt is married to long-time MSF Artistic Associate, Author, and Fight Director David Blixt, whom she met at the Festival in 1997 when they played Kate and Petruchio in *The Taming of the Shrew*. They are the parents of Dashiell and Evelyn.

# MICHIGAN Shakespeare FESTIVAL

Celebrating its 25th Season, The The Michigan Shakespeare Festival's mission is to inspire and entertain diverse audiences with evocative, interesting, and epic productions of classical theatre's greatest plays.

Originally the Jackson Shakespeare Festival, it started in 1995 as an outdoor summer event. A replica Globe was constructed in 1996, and in 1998 Artistic Director John Neville-Andrews changed the name to the Michigan Shakespeare Festival, reflecting the growing statewide poularity. Two years later the MSF added members of the Actor's Equity Association.

In 2003, the festival's growing reputation led the Michigan Senate to designate the MSF "The Official Shakespeare Festival of the State of Michigan." In 2004 the Festival moved to an indoors venue, taking up residence at the Potter Center at Jackson College.

In 2010 Janice L Blixt succeeded Neville-Andrews as the Artistic Director and a third classical play was added to the MainStage Season. At the same time the High School Tour was added, performing for students throughout the year in Michigan, Indiana, and Ohio.

In 2015, the Festival added a three-week run in Canton, MI, at the Village Theatre in Cherry Hill.

Now entering its 25th Anniversary Season, the MSF continues to grow, having entertained more than 100,000 patrons in its history.

FOR MORE INFORMATION, VISIT
WWW.MICHIGANSHAKESPEAREFESTIVAL.COM

## THE MYSTERY OF CENTRAL PARK

A rejected marriage proposal and the corpse of a dead beauty confound Dick Treadwell's hopes for happiness, until his beloved Penelope sets him a task: she will marry him if he solves—*the Mystery of Central Park!*

## EVA, THE ADVENTURESS

Nellie Bly's ripped-from-the-headlines novel of a poor girl determined to revenge herself upon the world, only to find that, in the battle between love and revenge, only one can triumph.

## NEW YORK BY NIGHT

Setting out to solve the bold diamond robbery, millionaire detective Lionel Dangerfield finds himself in competition with Ruby Sharpe, daring young reporter for the *New York Planet*. Will "The Danger" solve the case before Ruby can steal the story—and his heart?

## ALTA LYNN, M.D.

A prank goes awry and Alta Lynn finds herself wed against her will. Leaving love behind, she throws herself into the study of medicine, only to find that love has other plans for her!

## WAYNE'S FAITHFUL SWEETHEART

Beautiful Dorette Lover is rescued from poverty when she finds work as an artist's model. That same day she witnesses a seeming murder. To protect the man accused, she agrees to become his bride — only to fall desperately in love with him!

## LITTLE LUCKIE

Luckie Thurlow longs for to be accepted by society and gain the man she loves. But she harbors a dark secret — she is the daughter of the murderous Gypsy Queen, who plans to use Luckie to gain her own revenge!

## IN LOVE WITH A STRANGER

Kit Clarendon is in love! Trouble is, she doesn't know her love's name. But she is determined to track him down and force him to love her! A wild pursuit filled with disguises, desperate deeds, and declarations of love as Kit determines to go through fire and water to win him!

## THE LOVE OF THREE GIRLS

An heiress in disguise, a factory girl with dreams of wealth, and a sweet child of charity are forced into rivalry when they all fall in love with the same man! Murder, fever, fallen women, and a desperate villain conspire against —
*the love of three girls!*

## INTO THE MADHOUSE

Never before collected! "Who is this insane girl?" asked other papers, completely taken in by Nellie Bly's plan to infiltrate Blackwell's Island. The complete reporting surrounding her daring expose, including details not included in her initial accounts and her scathing rebuttal of the doctors' excuses!

## NELLIE BLY'S WORLD - Vol. 1
### 1887-1888

Bly's complete reporting, collected for the very first time! Starting with the stunt that made hers a household name, Nellie Bly spends her first year at the New York World going undercover to expose frauds, sharpsters and boodlers, interviewing Belva Lockwood and Hangman Joe, and tackling Phelps the Lobbyist!

## NELLIE BLY'S WORLD - Vol. 2
### 1889-1890

Bly's complete reporting, collected for the very first time! Nellie buys a baby, has herself followed by a detective and arrested, interviews Helen Keller, champion boxer John Sullivan, and convicted would-be killer Eva Hamilton, all before setting out on her greatest stunt of all, a race around the world!

## COMING SOON:

# NELLIE BLY'S WORLD, Vol. 3 & 4
# NELLIE BLY'S DISPATCHES, Vol. 1 & 2
# NELLIE BLY's JOURNALS, Vol. 1 & 2

### ALL FROM SORDELET INK

# Books by David Blixt

## Nellie Bly
What Girls Are Good For
Charity Girl
Clever Girl

## The Star-Cross'd Series
The Master Of Verona
Voice Of The Falconer
Fortune's Fool
The Prince's Doom
Varnish'd Faces: Star-Cross'd Short Stories

## Will & Kit
Her Majesty's Will

## The Colossus Series
Colossus: Stone & Steel
Colossus: The Four Emperors

Eve of Ides - a play

## Non-Fiction
Shakespeare's Secrets: Romeo & Juliet
Tomorrow, and Tomorrow: Essays on Macbeth
Fighting Words

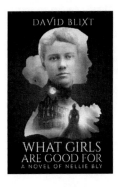

# WHAT GIRLS ARE GOOD FOR
## *A NOVEL OF NELLIE BLY*

Nellie Bly has the story of a lifetime. But will she survive to tell it?

Based on the real-life events of the tiny Pennsylvania spitfire who refused to let the world change her, and changed the world instead.

# CHARITY GIRL
## *A NELLIE BLY NOVELETTE*

Fresh from her escape from Blackwell's Island, Nellie Bly investigates the doctors who buy and sell babies in Victorian New York. Based on real events and her own reporting, Nellie Bly asks the devastating question—what becomes of babies?

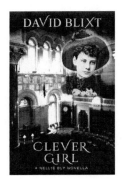

# CLEVER GIRL
## *A NELLIE BLY NOVELLA*

A blizzard has frozen all of New York, and Nellie Bly is going stir-crazy when she and Colonel Cockerill plot out her most daring undercover assignment yet: she's going to trap the most crooked man in politics, Edward R. Phelps, the self-styled "King" of the Albany lobby.

# COMING SOON:

# STUNT GIRL
## *A NOVEL OF NELLIE BLY*
### BY DAVID BLIXT

# Other Plays From SORDELET INK

**Action Movie - The Play** BY JOE FOUST AND RICHARD RAGSDALE

**All Childish Things** BY JOSEPH ZETTELMAIER

**Captain Blood** ADAPTED BY DAVID RICE

**the Count of Monte Cristo** ADAPTED BY CHRISTOPHER M. WALSH

**Dead Man's Shoes** BY JOSEPH ZETTELMAIER

**The Decade Dance** BY JOSEPH ZETTELMAIER

**Ebenezer: a christmas play** BY JOSEPH ZETTELMAIER

**Eve of Ides** BY DAVID BLIXT

**The Gravedigger: a frankenstein play** BY JOSEPH ZETTELMAIER

**Hatfield & McCoy** BY SHAWN PFAUTSCH

**Her Majesty's Will** ADAPTED BY ROBERT KAUZLARIC

**It Came From Mars** BY JOSEPH ZETTELMAIER

**the Moonstone** ADAPTED BY ROBERT KAUZLARIC

**Northern Aggression** BY JOSEPH ZETTELMAIER

**Once A Ponzi Time** BY JOE FOUST

**The Renaissance Man** BY JOSEPH ZETTELMAIER

**The Scullery Maid** BY JOSEPH ZETTELMAIER

**Season on the Line** BY SHAWN PFAUTSCH

**Stage Fright: a horror anthology** BY JOSEPH ZETTELMAIER

**a Tale of Two Cities** ADAPTED BY CHRISTOPHER M. WALSH

**Williamston Anthology: Volume 1**

**Williamston Anthology: Volume 2**

## WWW.SORDELETINK.COM

Made in United States
North Haven, CT
07 September 2023